With Blessings,

1/1/2014

What You Need To Know About *Marriage*

Julius Agbor Agbor, Ph.D.

WESTBOW
PRESS
A DIVISION OF THOMAS NELSON

Scripture Quotations were taken from the following three Bible Translations:

King James Version (KJV): No copyright information available.

Amplified Bible (AMP): "Scripture quotations taken from the Amplified® Bible, Copyright © 1954, 1958, 1962, 1964, 1965, 1987 by The Lockman Foundation. Used by permission." (www.Lockman.org)

The Message Bible (MSG): "Scripture taken from The Message. Copyright © 1993, 1994, 1995, 1996, 2000, 2001, 2002. Used by permission of NavPress Publishing Group."

WestBow Press books may be ordered through booksellers or by contacting:

WestBow Press
A Division of Thomas Nelson
1663 Liberty Drive
Bloomington, IN 47403
www.westbowpress.com
1 (866) 928-1240

ISBN: 978-1-4908-0920-5 (sc)
ISBN: 978-1-4908-0922-9 (hc)
ISBN: 978-1-4908-0921-2 (e)
Library of Congress Control Number: 2013916962

Printed in the United States of America.

WestBow Press rev. date: 09/25/2013

Table of Contents

Dedication.. vii

Foreword..ix

Preface xiii

Introduction xxi

Chapter 1   Marriage Is God's Idea 1

Chapter 2   The Decision to Marry 7

Chapter 3   Is Marriage For Everyone?............26

Chapter 4   Spouses Marital Obligations 32

Chapter 5   Does God Endorse Divorce? 49

Chapter 6   Problematic Situations 54

Chapter 7   Parents' Role in Their
            Children's Marriage Decision........66

Chapter 8   The Consequences of Marital
            Unfaithfulness 80

Chapter 9   Epilogue...87

About the Author 97

Dedication

This book is dedicated to two sets of people. First, it is dedicated to my parents, especially to my late Dad, Agbor Frederick Enoh, for training me as a kid in the way of the Lord. Second, it is dedicated to all my biological and spiritual children around the world, for believing in my mentorship.

Foreword

By Dr. Cheryl A. Hill[*]

Dr. Agbor is a man who balances practical living and godly principles. The title of this book gives you an idea of what you are in for as you read. It absolutely gives you "what you need to know." Many times we look for deep revelatory answers about our life's direction. We seek the advice of friends, family and even counselors. There is nothing wrong with seeking advice. What I love about Dr. Agbor's book is that he gives advice and

---

[*] *Dr. Cheryl A. Hill, author of "Godly Significance in the Marketplace," has 15 years of pastoring experience in the U.S. and is currently the President of Integrity International Consulting Group, LLC. In this capacity, she is a Special Advisor to a growing number of foreign Heads of State and to several U.S. governmental and faith leaders. Recently, she has served as Secretary of African Affairs at the UNESCO Center for Peace.*

direction, but most of all he leads you directly to "the source" which is God.

Marriage is such a gift in life and I believe if you begin grounded in the Word of God that you will live a complete and satisfying life with your assigned mate. Many times we want God in our lives, but only when it feels good to us. Sometimes the process of waiting or choosing your mate comes with difficult decisions, such as a conflict of feelings versus what God has set in place for you.

This book will provide a roadmap to a great marriage "if" you truly want God's best for you. Dr. Agbor has heard from God and therefore has written steps for you to go by and he teaches you to seek God for your answer.

I commend Dr. Agbor and recommend this book to those of you who sense God is calling you to marriage. Do not miss the instructions to healthy living and a healthy marriage. May God bless the work of the hands of Dr. Agbor and bless those of you who read this book; hear God and then move towards what God has said.

For the women who read this book "remember" that you are not the one who will seek your mate. It is the man that God will instruct to pursue you and you will know him by the leading of the Holy Spirit.

Whoso findeth a wife findeth a good thing, and obtaineth favor of the Lord. Proverbs 18:22 (KJV)

Preface

The idea of a book on marriage came to me as a revelation from God in the summer of 2011. My wife Belinda and I had just concluded a day's fast, on the occasion of our 10th wedding anniversary. Prior to this, we had just relocated into the United States with our three kids. We had heard many stereotypes about the United States. Amongst them, the notion that marriages hardly last in the United States and born-again Christians tend to divorce at almost the same rate as non-Christians.

Indeed, the statistics strongly support these views. For instance, a March 2008 study by the Barna Group, suggests that though marriage has been the norm in the United States, about one-third

(33 percent) of adults who have been married had experienced at least one divorce. Most strikingly are the findings that in matters of divorce, born-again Christians were indistinguishable from the national average: 33 percent have been married and divorced! With increasing globalization, it would be hard to refute that this divorce trend in the United States is internationalizing. If you have doubts, just take a look at the rate at which the phenomenon of gay marriages is being endorsed globally.

As a development economist whose fundamental research agenda is to provide practical solutions that could contribute to poverty alleviation around the world, I am disturbed by these statistics on divorce rates, most especially as recent scientific studies have established a clear link between poverty and the growth in single-parent households in the United States.

To the extent that most single-parent households are the fruit of divorce not death, it is fair to claim a link between poverty and divorce. For instance, a local report in the Ozarks News has shown that one of every two single mothers lives in poverty. If these divorce repercussions only affected poverty rates, that would be dramatic enough, but research findings show that other important societal dimensions are also negatively affected. For instance, studies by the Single Parent Success Foundation reveal that a child in a single-parent household is far more likely to experience violence, commit suicide, continue a cycle of poverty, become drug dependent, commit a crime or perform below his peers in education.

Following my fast in the summer of 2011, the Lord's message to me was very clear: "I want you to write a book on marriage. This is because solidifying the family structure—through properly established marriages—is the key not only to poverty reduction but also to better functioning communities." The Lord told me to tell the world that He is the one who created the marriage institution and there is a specific divine pattern to be followed.

Having learnt to walk intimately with the Lord for almost a decade, I had no doubt in my heart that the Lord wanted me to write this book, but what I didn't know at the time was how soon He wanted it done. So I simply noted down the instruction as one of those things I would do at some stage in life, probably after my 50th wedding anniversary, if Jesus still hasn't come. Why the procrastination? Because I had been deceived in my mind—temporarily though—that a very long successful married life, or a proven track record of successful marriage counseling experience are the necessary credentials to author a book on marriage.

But Scriptures show us this way of thinking isn't consistent with God's ways of operating. For instance, the Apostle Paul wasn't one of the 12 disciples who walked with Jesus but his revelation of Jesus Christ—as evidenced by the number of books he wrote in the New Testament—is arguably deeper than many of the other 12 apostles. In fact, the Apostle Peter—who walked with Jesus—confessed in one of his epistles his inability to comprehend some of the things which Paul wrote about Jesus. Isn't this an amazing testimony about someone who never met Jesus physically all through Jesus' ministry on earth? What this tells us is that God can use anyone to accomplish His divine purpose on earth. All that is needed is an obedient and willing heart.

During my personal bible study times over the past two years, the leadings of the Spirit have been frequently for me to study Scriptures on marriage. And often in my prayer times, the Lord would impress in my heart the Scripture in 2 Timothy 20-21 (MSG):

> "In a well-furnished kitchen there are not only crystal goblets and silver platters, but waste cans and compost buckets— some containers used to serve fine meals, others to take out the garbage. Become the kind of container God can use to present any and every kind of gift to His guests for their blessing."

Many a time, the resounding message from that Scripture which would flow through my spirit and thoughts is: "I want someone I can use as a vessel in order to deliver an important message to the church and world." I heard the call to write this book and I have responded to it. Your own responsibility is to study this book diligently because the Lord has something in store for you in it. It doesn't matter whether you are a Christian, Muslim, Buddhist or an atheist. This book has something for you. My prayer for you as you read this book is that the eyes of your understanding will be enlightened to receive all that God has in store for you!

At this time, some acknowledgments are in order. I want to first seize this opportunity to thank the Lord for the life of my spiritual parents, Bishop Dr. Winston and Charmaine Pienaar of Restoration Life Ministry, Cape Town, South Africa, through whom I received Christ. I also would like to express my sincere appreciation to my spiritual mentor, Rev. Pastor Chris Oyakhilome, Ph.D., President of Believers' LoveWorld Inc. (a.k.a. Christ Embassy) for the sound teaching in the Word of God, which I have received as a son in the house over the past five years. Because of Pastor Chris, I know who I am in Christ. Thank you so much Pastor Chris for being a great blessing to me and to the world.

To my lovely wife, Belinda Obi Agbor, I want to acknowledge the very special place you occupy in my heart, and I thank you so much for helping to bring out the best in me so that I can be a blessing to others. A special word of thanks goes to my junior brother, Emmanuel Oben Agbor, for providing the initial financial support to kick start this project, without which it might not have seen the light of day. I say to my children: Dorcas, Fred Clancy, Paul Richnel and Chrisma Esther, that my life wouldn't be complete without each one of you in it.

Introduction

What You Need to Know about Marriage is a response to a call by God to enlighten both the Church of Jesus Christ and the world at large, on the subject of marriage. As such, this book is specially written with several categories of folks in mind. For folks currently contemplating a marriage or divorce decision, or those in problematic marriage situations, this is the book you have been waiting for. This book will also serve as an invaluable resource for parents, Church ministers and marriage counselors.

Being an inspiration from God, all the material you will find in this book is referenced from the written Word of God that is contained in the Holy Scriptures. My earnest endeavor in this book has been to accurately convey as much as possible, the revelations given to me by the Spirit of God. The way I go about achieving this is by weighing my personal revelations on this subject against the written Word, since Scripture cannot be broken. I invite you to diligently cross-check the Scriptures with me as you read this book. You will notice that most of my Scripture references are quoted from the Message Bible. This is mainly because of its simplicity.

The book is organized into 9 chapters, each chapter addressing a specific topic. Chapter One sets the pace by arguing that marriage is God's idea, not man's and God construed marriage to be between a man and a woman. It argues further that, in marriage, the man and his wife are to become "one flesh," which literally means they are supposed to have a consistent common approach to life, in spite of whatever differences might exist between them.

Since marriage is God's idea, God certainly has laid out principles in His Word for how marriage should be approached: this is the subject matter of Chapter Two of this book. In particular, Chapter Two dwells on such issues as: "Should the man or the woman make the first move in a marriage proposition? What factors should one consider when making a marriage decision? Does belonging to a different race, tribe or religion matter in the marriage decision?"

Chapter Three answers some very pertinent questions amongst many Christian folk today, notably, whether marriage is for everyone. It also addresses such questions as whether a life of celibacy is superior to a married life in terms of service to God, and whether it is sinful to abandon an initially proclaimed life of celibacy.

Chapter Four specifically targets married folks. It addresses four important marital obligations of spouses as endorsed in God's Word, namely, the obligation to remain married, the obligation to remain faithful, the obligation to love and the obligation of submission.

In the light of the alarming divorce rates both in the Church and in the world today, many aren't exactly sure what God's perspective on divorce is. Chapter Five provides an in-depth scriptural answer to this question. In particular, it dwells on the issue of whether it is scripturally right to divorce on grounds of marital unfaithfulness.

Although God's Word has laid out principles on how marriage should be organized, many folks, including believing Christians, often do not get it right. Chapter Six addresses some of the problematic marriage situations that arise because one of the parties to a marriage is saved and the other isn't—what has been biblically termed a 'mixed marriage.' It addresses such questions as: "Is it biblical for a believing spouse to divorce his/her unbelieving spouse? What kind of prayer brings about the salvation of a loved one or spouse? What's the appropriate conduct to adopt when an unbelieving spouse quits? What are the consequences when believing spouses divorce?" These are just a few questions, amongst others.

In perilous times such as we live in today, many parents have lost influence over their children's marriage decisions. Worse still, some parents aren't aware that they are supposed to play a role in shaping their children's marriage decisions. Some attempt to influence their children's choices very late—when these children are already grown up and matured—with disastrous consequences.

Another category is when parents aren't even aware that their children are already married. All of these stem from the fact that many parents haven't assumed their proper scriptural role in the upbringing of their children. Chapter Seven dwells into parents' role, not only in raising their kids, but also in their future marital decisions.

Under the dispensation of grace which Christ Jesus ushered us into, many Christian folks have a hard time complying with the message of the Old Testament. For instance, does grace invalidate the sin in fornication and marital unfaithfulness? Chapter Eight answers these questions by expounding on the consequences of marital unfaithfulness. Chapter Nine puts together my main thoughts developed in this book and offer the unsaved reader an opportunity to receive salvation in Jesus Christ.

Chapter One

Marriage Is God's Idea

*"God, not you, made marriage. His Spirit inhabits
even the smallest details of marriage. And what
does He want from marriage? Children of God,
that's what. So guard the spirit of marriage
within you. Don't cheat on your spouse."*
Malachi 2:15 (MSG)

This Scripture makes it explicitly clear that
marriage is God's idea, not man's idea. When
God finished creating the universe, He also created
man and put him in the garden called Eden. In
Genesis 2:15-17, God gave explicit instructions to
man regarding keeping the Garden of Eden: what
man was allowed and not allowed to eat and the

consequences that would follow for breaking the instruction.

By then, only the man existed; God had not yet created the woman. Genesis 2:18 tells us that God didn't find it proper for the man to be alone, and He thus created the woman to be the man's helper or companion. We draw from the preceding that the mission to cater for the Garden of Eden was originally assigned to the man *alone;* and when God later brought the woman into the scene, it was for the purpose of assisting or supporting the man in accomplishing his predetermined assignment. To allow us stay focused on the subject matter of this chapter, we will postpone the discussion of the role of the man and woman in marriage to the next chapter.

God was explicit about how the relationship between the man and the woman should be.

He wanted them to be one, unified in marriage. Genesis 2:24 (KJV) says:

"Therefore shall a man leave his father and mother, and shall cleave unto his wife: and they shall be one flesh."

The Hebrew word translated *flesh* in this verse is *bâsâr*, which means body or person. It is very clear from this Scripture that God purposed for the man to someday leave his father and mother and be joined together to his wife and that the man and his wife were to become one person.

Notice again in Genesis 2:24 that the marriage instruction is given explicitly to the man to leave behind his biological family. Of course, this doesn't suggest that the married woman should hold tight to her own biological family, because she and her husband are expected to become one person.

Oneness of person here does not necessarily suggest that there will be no differences between the husband and wife when it comes to decision-making. There will always be differences in thought and approach, but God expects the married couple to always come to a compromise based on Scripture. For instance, if one person likes hanging out at parties with friends but the other dislikes it, the couple must not allow these divergent lifestyles to entrench, because sooner than later, it would jeopardize the marriage. What they have to do is to seek reconciliation of their different perspectives through the Word of God.

The Bible is the standard or principle by which a Christian marriage abides. This is why it is extremely important for couples to grow in knowledge of the Word of God. God expects the husband and the wife to have a consistent common approach to life. Thus, if one party has a *biblical* reason for disliking something, the other party is also compelled by the rule of marriage to dislike it. Note that the compromise ought to be made in favor of the party who has a valid scriptural basis and not on the basis of male chauvinism or financial power. That is what it means to have a consistent common approach to life.

There are some married men who haven't left behind their biological families in the sense that their parents, especially their mothers, are still patronizing their decisions. This is wrong, according to Scripture, and no sooner will such marriages hit the rocks because instead of being one person with his wife, the man has chosen to be one person with his mother!

In summary, marriage is a God-ordained idea between a man and a woman. If God ordained marriages, then He must have some rules and principles by which they should abide. The Word of God is the standard or principle by which a marriage should function properly. This means that couples are required to have a sound knowledge of God's Word. Without a sound knowledge of God's Word, they wouldn't be able to properly apply the wisdom of God to situations that they need to address. Couples are bound to face divergent opinions and approaches in life, but they are expected to use God's Word in reconciling their differences.

Chapter Two

The Decision to Marry

"Therefore shall a man leave his father and mother, and shall cleave unto his wife: and they shall be one flesh."
Genesis 2:24 (KJV)

Having acknowledged the fact that marriage is God's idea and that God has laid out principles by which a marriage should function, we are now ready to consider the marriage decision. In this chapter, we answer the following three questions: Who should make the marriage proposition? What are the factors to consider when making a marriage decision? Does belonging to a different race, tribe, or religion affect the marriage decision?

From our theme Scripture above, it is clear that the man is supposed to initiate the marriage proposition and not the other way around. God does not expect the woman to make a marriage proposition to the man. However, before the man proposes to the woman, the Scripture (Genesis 2:15-17) tells us that he must have first and foremost understood the assignment given to him by God. Even before the woman came onto the scene, God had mandated the man for specific assignments, generically described in Genesis 2:15 (MSG) as "working the ground and keeping it in order."

In the context of today, these assignments refer to the many different callings or vocations through which God manifests Himself to our world. Some folks are called into the fivefold ministry (namely, apostles, prophets, evangelists, pastors, and teachers), while others are called into the lay ministry (that is, to keep their secular vocations while simultaneously carrying out their priestly ministry). Various professionals such as accountants, physicians, lawyers, professors, and you name the rest, can thus be included in the category of lay ministers. The fivefold ministry thus primarily distinguishes itself from the lay ministry in that it is frequently a full-time occupation for those called into it. Notwithstanding, it is also not uncommon to find lay ministers who are functioning in different offices as pastors, evangelists, or teachers of God's Word.

It is, however, important to note that neither the fivefold nor the lay ministry is a permanent outcome for anyone. Some folks start out in the lay ministry and wind up in the fivefold ministry and vice versa. Whether in the fivefold or lay ministry, the underlying fact of the matter is that every Christian is called to be involved in spreading the gospel of Jesus Christ.

After a man has identified his specific calling in Christ, God generally wants him to accomplish this with the help of a woman. Sometimes, the woman may have an original assignment from God, for God is no respecter of persons, but usually such cases are the exception rather than the rule. In any case, to the extent that the two intending parties to a marriage are able to work together in their respective callings, they can enter a marital relationship. We will come back in more detail to this discussion in the next chapter.

In general, God gives the assignment to the man who, in line with the requirements of his specific assignment, looks for the specific woman who will ensure his success at the God-given assignment.

The preceding suggests that a man ought to make a marriage proposition to the woman only after he has fully grasped and understood his specific calling in Christ. Otherwise, how is he to know the specific qualities of the wife to look for?

For instance, the qualities desired of a pastor's wife are quite different from those desired of a lay minister's wife. In particular, pastors' wives are generally women who themselves have been called into the fivefold ministry. The reason some have failed in life is either because they chose the wrong person in marriage or because they never really understood their God-given assignment and were therefore busy mimicking other people's callings.

If you have been called into the fivefold ministry, then your ideal partner in marriage should be someone with a similar calling. This should be the one non-negotiable attribute to look out for.

Ironically, for those who are called into the lay ministry, the qualities of a marriage partner are sometimes more difficult to discern. This is because of the likelihood of one or both spouses eventually entering into the fivefold ministry at some later stage.

As the first mover in a marriage proposition, we now discuss four essential attributes that a man should look out for in a potential wife.

The Four Essential Attributes of a Wife

The first and most important attribute of a potential wife is inner beauty. 1 Peter 3:1-4 (MSG) summarizes this as follows:

> **"The same goes for you wives: be good wives to your husbands, responsive to**

their needs. There are husbands who, indifferent as they are to any words about God, will be captivated by your life of holy beauty. What matters is not your outer appearance—the styling of your hair, the jewelry you wear, the cut of your clothes—but your inner disposition. Cultivate inner beauty, the gentle, gracious kind that God delights in."

Inner beauty comes from a renewed spirit. A renewed spirit comes after one accepts Jesus Christ as Lord and Savior (that is, becomes born again) and is filled with the Holy Spirit. A woman who is born again and filled with the Holy Spirit is also full of wisdom, which makes her a suitable help mate for the husband. The wisdom I am referring to here is not the wisdom of scholars or the wisdom that comes with ageing, both of which are limited.

Rather, this is about divine wisdom or the wisdom of God. The wisdom of God gives insight into reality. That is, the ability to provide time-tested solutions to complex and challenging situations. It is the ability both to know and to do the right thing the first time. This is a gift which only God can give. Science, even at its best, is unable to deliver this kind of wisdom.

The Scriptures are replete with examples of men and women who have demonstrated this kind of wisdom but due to limited space, I will highlight only the case of Queen Esther here. This is recorded for us in the book of Esther 3:13 (MSG):

> "Bulletins were sent out by couriers to all the King's provinces with orders to massacre, kill, and eliminate all the Jews-youngsters and old men, women and babies—on a single day, the thirteenth

day of the twelfth month, the month
Adar, and to plunder their goods"

As the story goes, there was a conspiracy—backed by official orders—to assassinate all Jews in the Kingdom of Xerxes and every detail, including the date for the operation was all set. Thus, in the physical realm, absolutely nothing was standing in the way of execution of the King's order to annihilate the Jews. The only way the Jews could escape this impending genocide was if Queen Esther obtained leniency from the King but to do that, she would have to bear the risk of appearing before the King without the King's invitation. As expected, this option had deathly consequences for the Scripture record that anyone who dared appear uninvited before the King had only one outcome: death, unless the King showed leniency.

The stakes were thus high for Queen Esther. If she appeared uninvited before the King, not only would she be risking her life but also, all her Jewish kinsmen were going to be slaughtered according to the program that was in place. How on earth did Queen Esther know what to do in this situation? She probably had consulted with the royal experts of the day who must have discouraged the idea of her petitioning the King on the matter. Mind you, the wisdom of experts' is not always accurate. Yet, thanks to the wisdom of God, a viable solution—which contradicts the expert opinion on the problem—was found. Queen Esther instructed all her kinsmen to undertake a three-day fast prior to her unscheduled appointment with the King. When she finally met with the King, not only did the King spare her life, but deliverance also came to all the Jewish people. Remarkable! We observe therefore that the fast was the game-changer in that life threatening situation. But how on earth did Queen Esther know this was what needed to be done? That is the wisdom of God I'm talking about!

The second most important attribute of a potential wife is intelligence. It is commonly accepted that intelligence is sexy. Someone can be wise yet not be intelligent and vice versa. To be intelligent means to possess the aptitude to think critically, to argue broadly and coherently, and to be able to present one's ideas in a clear, orderly, and systematic manner. Intelligence is gained from secular education. Unlike wisdom, which comes from an understanding of the Word of God, intelligence comes from secular education. Intelligent women are also generally top-achievers and women who are well able to support their families financially and otherwise.

The third most important attribute of a potential wife is a submissive heart or character. Several Scriptures emphasize submission as a critical requirement expected of women in marriage. Ephesians 5: 22-24 (KJV) says:

> "Wives, submit yourselves unto your own husbands, as unto the Lord . . . therefore as the church is subject unto Christ, so let the wives be to their own husbands in every thing."

Colossians 3:18 (KJV) re-echoes the same message:

> "Wives, submit yourselves unto your own husbands, as it is fit in the Lord."

We know as a spiritual principle, that whenever the Spirit of God says something over and over again, it means that it is absolutely important. Again, the very fact that men are generally more inclined to adoring women who submit to their authority as opposed to women who oppose them, is proof positive of the importance of submission.

But someone might ask: how in the world am I supposed to discern whether my potential wife will be submissive to me? I will give you a clue. As a rule of thumb, ladies who aren't submissive to their own parents—biological and spiritual—will generally have a hard time submitting to anyone else, including their husbands. Some investigation into the background of the potential wife, specifically in respect to her character, is thus mandated.

The fourth most important attribute to look for in a wife is outward or physical beauty. These refer to attractive physical qualities like facial looks, body structure, tone, etc. They would also include little things like charm and personal hygiene. The specific physical characteristics desired for in a wife are sensitive to individual appreciation so we will not dwell much into that.

Now I can sense someone questioning, but what if my fiancé doesn't have all four of those qualities? Should I ditch her? My advice is this: go ahead with your marriage plans as long as your fiancé meets at least the first most important quality, which is inner beauty. After you are married, both of you can work on refining the remaining three qualities. This is because the single quality of being born-again and filled with the spirit of God predisposes anyone for success in every area of life. If worked on, inner beauty of the spirit will eventually manifest itself on the outside, sharpen one's intelligence and mold one into a submissive wife.

While the preceding discussion has focused mainly on the parameters for judging a suitable wife, they equally apply in evaluating a suitable husband, with the only difference being that the man's submission is primarily to God and not to his wife. How can we observe a man's submission to God? When he listens to what God's Word says and does it. This is because God and His Word are inseparable: you cannot claim to be submissive to God's authority when you aren't submissive to the authority of His Word in your life. Over and above the four essential attributes discussed above, a man who is ready to make a marriage proposition must already have a clear understanding of his specific God-given assignment.

Now let's turn to the question of whether belonging to a different race, tribe or religion affects the marriage decision. To answer this question, we need to recognize the difference between the dispensation of the law as it applied to Israel and the dispensation of grace as it applies to the Church of Jesus Christ.

Under the dispensation of the law, the children of Israel were expressly instructed to marry only within their tribes or clans for the reason of protecting the tribal land inheritance (see Numbers 36). Interestingly, though, in the new dispensation of the Church of Jesus Christ, the *intra-tribal* marriage instruction still holds, but the difference is in the definition and delimitation of the term "tribe."

It is important to recognize that the term "tribe" in the Church dispensation has a different meaning from the law dispensation. In the law dispensation— which corroborates well with the present day secular interpretation—the term "tribe" describes people of a common natural or ancestral origin. Examples include, the Jewish tribe, the Philistines and also all the various micro-ethnic groups in different countries around the world. In the Church dispensation, however, God sees the entire world as divided into only two main tribes namely, the heavenly and the earthy tribe:

> "The First Man was made out of earth, and people since then are earthy; the Second Man was made out of heaven, and people now can be heavenly. In the same way that we've worked from our earthy origins, let's embrace our heavenly ends." 1 Cor. 15:48-49 (MSG)

The heavenly tribe is composed of all those who have their origin from the Second and last Adam—who is Jesus Christ. Thus, the heavenly tribe is the Church of Jesus Christ—which includes everyone who is born-again—irrespective of color, race or linguistic background. God sees the entire Church of Jesus Christ as one race and a nation of its own.

1 Peter 2:9 (AMP) says:

> "But you are a chosen race, a royal
> priesthood, a dedicated nation . . ."

The earthy tribe is composed of all those who
have their origin from the First Adam. In other
words, they are those who aren't born again.
God's injunction against *inter-tribal* marriages
still applies to our day. 2 Cor. 6:14 (MSG) says:

> "Don't become partners with those
> who reject God. How can you make
> a partnership out of right and wrong?
> That's not partnership; that's war. Is
> light best friends with dark?"

Therefore, we see that from God's perspective,
marriage between the heavenly and the earthy
tribe is an aberration. The implication of this is
that a born-again Christian shouldn't enter into a

marriage relationship with someone who doesn't have Jesus Christ as Lord and Savior.

Some folks may argue that what if marrying an unbeliever leads to their salvation, wouldn't that be an acceptable reason? The answer is simple: such folk believe they are wiser than God. God, in His infinite wisdom, has laid out the procedure for winning unbelievers to Christ. The Word of God clearly instructs us to preach the gospel as the means of bringing salvation to all men and women. No where is it recommended in Scripture that we should marry unbelievers in order to save them. In fact, the Word tells us in John 3:18 that anyone who does not believe in Jesus Christ is already condemned; so where is the wisdom in marrying such a person, other than that you are also seeking to destroy yourself?

Chapter Three

Is Marriage For Everyone?

*"Sometimes I wish everyone were single like
me—a simpler life in many ways! But celibacy
is not for everyone any more than marriage
is. God gives the gift of the single life to some,
the gift of the married life to others."*
1 Cor. 7:7 (MSG)

The Apostle Paul, by inspiration of the Spirit of
God, makes clear in our theme Scripture above
that marriage, like celibacy, is not for everyone.
Though we have argued in the previous chapters
that it is God's desire for the man to be supported
in his divine assignment by a woman, the fact that
there may be instances where a woman herself is

given an original assignment by God, suggests that marriage is not mandatory for everyone. In fact, the Apostle Paul suggests that there is a special grace to be married and a special grace to live single because each condition has its specific challenges.

The married person faces several distractions from regularly seeking to please his spouse, family and in-laws, which is time that could be devoted in service to the Lord.

Further, when you marry, you take on additional stress in an already stressful world, which is why the Apostle Paul goes to the extreme of recommending celibacy, if possible. The idea is to avoid unnecessary complications in life so that one can be more focused on his/her divine assignment to accomplish it.

In spite of this imperative, and though himself single, the Apostle Paul makes a strong case for marriage suggesting that the benefits thereof, in terms of sexual sanity, far exceed the problems engendered by being single and sexually disoriented:

> "But if they can't manage their desires and emotions, they should by all means go ahead and get married. The difficulties of marriage are preferable by far to a sexually tortured life as a single." 1Cor. 7:9 (MSG)

In addition, the Apostle Paul shows us that marriage is spiritually and morally right and is not inferior to celibacy in any way, although he has pastoral reasons for encouraging singleness because of the times we live in, 1 Cor. 7:38 (MSG).

Notwithstanding, the Scripture in 1 Cor. 7:37 show us that if anyone is comfortable in his/her decision for a single life in service to God and as long as that decision is purely a personal conviction and not something that is imposed on him/her by others, then he/she ought to stick with it. The Apostle Paul, like our Savior Jesus Christ, lived a single life yet was able to satisfactorily fulfill his divine assignment without reproach. Therefore a life of celibacy in service to God is highly esteemable and something worth pursuing.

However, as noted in our theme Scripture, the grace for that is not given to everyone of us. Many of us aren't able to contain our sexual drives, which is why the Scriptures admonish us to marry:

> ". . . Sexual drives are strong but marriage is strong enough to contain them and provide for a balanced and fulfilling sexual life in a world of sexual disorder . . ." 1 Cor. 7:2 (MSG)

In summary, four key messages standout in this chapter. The first is that God places a high premium on the fulfillment of the divine assignment by each one of us. Since we are all different, not only in our capabilities, but also in our emotional resolve, God gives special grace for marriage to some and special grace for celibacy to others.

The second key message is that celibacy as an act of service to God isn't superior to marriage. The third key message is that celibacy has two important constrains associated with it: it's a life entirely dedicated to God's service and in which sexual activity is intolerable.

The fourth key message is that celibacy isn't necessarily a lock-in situation that can not be reversed, unlike marriage which can be reversed only after the death of a spouse. We will come back to the issue of marriage separation in a later chapter. Thus, if someone had earlier made up his/her mind not to get married but finds it difficult to stick to that decision, the Scriptures show that he/she can go ahead and get married. No sin is committed in getting married against one's initial self-imposed life of celibacy:

> "If a man has a woman friend to whom he is loyal but never intended to marry, having decided to serve God as a 'single,' and then changes his mind, deciding he should marry her, he should go ahead and marry. It's no sin; it's not even a 'step down' from celibacy, as some say."
> 1 Cor. 7:36 (MSG)

Chapter Four

Spouses Marital Obligations

This chapter addresses four important marital obligations of spouses, as endorsed in God's Word, namely, the obligation to remain married, the obligation to remain faithful, the obligation to love and the obligation of submission.

The obligation is to remain married for life.

"I hate divorce," says the God of Israel. God-of-the-Angel-Armies says, "I hate the violent dismembering of the 'one flesh' of marriage." So watch yourselves. Don't let your guard down. Don't cheat. Malachi 2:16 (MSG)

One of the fundamental spiritual principles of marriage is that spouses are required to remain married for life. The marriage contract has no expiration date. It makes no difference how spouses feel towards each other, once married, there is no other scriptural option left but to remain committed to each other. Essentially, the marriage decision is crucially important because of its non-reversibility.

God sees the married couple as 'one flesh,' which is why He disgusts any "violent dismembering of the one flesh of marriage." The story of King Solomon and the two harlots who each claimed ownership of a son in 1 Kings 3 speaks volumes about God's attitude towards separation. King Solomon suggested as a compromise between the belligerent women to divide the baby into two equal halves, but the woman whose baby it truly was, rejected the proposition.

As the story goes, it is the woman who opposed separation (indeed, killing) of the 'one flesh' of the baby who triumphed in the case. Apparently, this is the same wisdom that is being employed by secular judges today when faced with a divorce case in which one of the spouses is against separation.

It is important to realize that God almighty is a silent witness when spouses make their marriage vows:

> ". . . Because God was there as a witness when you spoke your marriage vows to your young bride, and now you've broken those vows, broken the faith-bond with your vowed companion, your covenant wife." Malachi 2:14 (MSG)

Not only witnessing to the marriage vows, the Scriptures say in Malachi 2:15 that God's Spirit inhabits even the smallest details of marriage.

Some folks have put away their spouses because they no longer have the same feelings of love that they had when they got married. That is wrong and God will hold them accountable for that decision. You are not required to remain married because of unfaltering feelings. Feelings are subject to change, which is why no sensible person should base his/her marriage decision on feelings. Understand that marriage is an irrevocable vow made before God almighty and He expects you to keep it all the way through life.

There is an obligation to remain faithful.

"Honor marriage, and guard the sacredness of sexual intimacy between wife and husband. God draws a firm line against casual and illicit sex." Hebrews 13:4 (MSG)

Our theme Scripture above is clear: from a biblical perspective, sex is only permissible within a marriage setting. It is scripturally illegal outside the confines of marriage, including during courtship. Notice that the Scripture above does not suggest that sexual intimacy between a husband and several wives (and vice versa) is tolerated: because marriage on God's terms is between one man and one woman.

Sex is probably the only biblical instruction that changes with the marital status of the Christian. Before marriage, God's instruction is no sex. But right after the marriage ceremony has been performed, the instruction is keep at it, do not abstain without a valid spiritual reason:

> **"Abstaining from sex is permissible for a period of time if you both agree to it, and if it's for the purposes of prayer and**

fasting—but only for such times. Then come back together again. Satan has an ingenious way of tempting us when we least expect it." 1Cor. 7:5 (MSG)

It is worth emphasizing here that there are some things in the New Testament which the Apostle Paul wrote out of his own wise counsel, but weren't necessarily God's instruction to us. We know this because Paul himself admits this in the following verse:

> "I'm not, understand, commanding these periods of abstinence—only providing my best counsel if you should choose them." 1 Cor.7:6 (MSG).

Wisdom therefore tells us that abstinence from sex could equally be for other genuine scriptural reasons besides prayer and fasting. For instance, abstinence can also take place in order to avoid undesired pregnancies, especially if the couple isn't financially ready:

> "Is there anyone here who, on planning to build a new house, doesn't first sit down and figure the cost so you'll know if you can complete it? If you only get the foundation laid out and then run out of money, you're going to look pretty foolish. Everyone passing by will poke fun at you: 'he started something he couldn't finish.'" Luke 14:28-30 (MSG)

Modern technology, through various contraceptives, has even reduced the need for abstinence on grounds other than fasting and prayer. Contrary to what some Christian folks believe, there is nothing scripturally wrong with the use of contraceptives amongst married couples.

We observe therefore that although spouses are obligated to frequently satisfy each others' emotional and sexual desires, doing this all the time without wise planning is tantamount to foolishness:

> "All things are lawful for me, but all things are not expedient: all things are lawful for me, but all things edify not."
> 1 Cor.10:23 (KJV)

> "Likewise, ye husbands, dwell with them according to knowledge . . ."
> 1Peter 3:7 (KJV)

The obligation to love

> "Husbands, love your wives, even as Christ also loved the Church, and gave himself for it." Ephesians 5:25 (KJV)

According to the Scripture above, the obligation to love is expressly mandated to the husband. The 28th verse of the same Scripture continues in the same light:

> "So ought men to love their wives as their own bodies. He that loveth his wife loveth himself."

In emphasizing the love requirement to the husbands and not to the wives, it would appear that the Spirit of God has identified love as the crucial challenge in marriage that husbands' face.

The Scripture defines love for us in 1 Cor. 13:4-7 (MSG):

> "Love never gives up. Love cares more for others than for self. Love doesn't want what it doesn't have. Love doesn't strut, Doesn't have a swelled head, Doesn't

force itself on others, Isn't always "me first," Doesn't fly off the handle, Doesn't keep score of the sins of others, Doesn't revel when others grovel, Takes pleasure in the flowering of truth, Puts up with anything, Trusts God always, Always looks for the best, Never looks back, But keeps going to the end."

So much to be said and written on the above Scriptures but I believe they are self-explanatory. However, it suffices to note that a husband who loves his wife wouldn't give up on her, would show understanding and wouldn't demand from her what she doesn't have.

As simple as this sounds, it's amazing how many folks miss it! Oftentimes husbands think that their acts of giving and romantic words are sufficient demonstration of love to their wives. Some even think the fact that they are able to fully satisfy their wives' sexual desires is proof-positive of their love for them.

While all of these are important and certainly have their place in marriage, the scriptures show us that there is more to love than that. Simple things men take for granted like frequently citing the "good" qualities of other women isn't suggestive of love to their wives because every woman is unique in the way God created her.

Furthermore, if you find that the qualities in the other woman—which are not in your wife—are so overwhelmingly desirable to you, then the problem is definitely with you the husband and not with the wife. Your problem is that you are demanding from your wife what she doesn't have, whereas you are supposed to love her the way she is! You might have been led to marriage by the feelings you had for her but once married, you are required to love the woman you married, even if those feelings are no longer there.

Finally, a husband who loves his wife wouldn't insist on having things his own way; wouldn't remember all her wrongs and would always believe the best from her. Small wonder the Bible declares that love never fails!

The obligation of submission

Just as the obligation of love applies primarily to the husband, the obligation of submission applies primarily to the wife. As noted before, as head of the family, God expects the husband to be submissive to divine authority headed by God Himself; otherwise, the husband's authority over the family would be in jeopardy.

There are some folks who have a hard time getting their wife and children submit to their authority but what they don't realize is that before you can get anyone else submit to you, you have got to first submit yourself to God's authority. In other words, you have got to let the Word of God rule over your life.

Now to the wives, God says submit yourselves to your *own* husbands in *every thing*:

> "Wives, submit yourselves unto your own husbands, as unto the Lord . . . therefore as the church is subject unto Christ, so let the wives be to their own husbands in every thing." Ephesians 5:22-24 (KJV)

The word "submit" in the above scripture is translated from the Greek word "hupŏtassō" which means to subordinate one's self, to obey or be under obedience to another, or to be in subjection to another. Language scholars would tell us that to subordinate one's self means to bring one's self below another in rank or importance, or to be under the authority of another person.

Putting all these definitions together suggests that God wants the married woman—irrespective of her educational, family or financial status—to bring herself below her husband in rank/importance and to consistently stay under the authority of her husband in every thing.

It is therefore God's command for the woman to be under her husband's authority and rule. Wives listen, husbands didn't invent this command! God almighty Himself gave it. Genesis 3:16 (KJV) also emphasizes this point:

> "Unto the woman He said, I will greatly
> multiply thy sorrow and thy conception;
> in sorrow thou shall bring forth children;

and thy desire shall be to thy husband,

and he shall rule over thee."

Are you aware that this lone requirement explains why so many women who long to get married haven't yet found a spouse, and some who found one have divorced? Whether consciously or unconsciously, such women are looking for so-called "equality" with the man, but that is not the right attitude God expects from women in marriage.

Make no mistake, God knows that women also deserve dignity and I believe that is why God has not commanded married women to be submissive to every male person in the world. Had God commanded women to be submissive to the male folk, it would have amounted to subjugation but God isn't unjust. Rather, the Scripture instructs women to be submissive to their own husbands, who incidentally are supposed to already love them.

So there shouldn't be any loss of dignity in that! Therefore, only the husband should appreciate his wife's submission not anyone else, be it the father or mother-in-law, as is common in some cultures particularly in Africa. Of course, this is not to suggest that the wife should disrespect her parents-in-law.

Further, the wife's submission to her husband is not supposed to be a once-off affair or something she should do whenever she's happy or feels like it. The fact of the matter is that, more often than not, wives wouldn't feel like submitting to their husbands, yet they are required to do so, and on a consistent daily basis.

Because God created each one of us with an ego, submission shouldn't be expected to come naturally: rather, it is something to consciously and prayerfully practice. The fact that the scriptures emphasize wives' submission to their husbands over and over again should tell us that God is aware of the immense challenge that wives seeking to put this to work would face.

My final advice to married women is that, as daughters of Sarah, they should copy Sarah's attitude towards her husband, Abraham. Sarah obeyed Abraham to the extent of addressing him "my lord":

> **"Even as Sarah obeyed Abraham calling him lord: whose daughters ye are, as long as ye do well, and are not afraid with any amazement." 1Peter 3:6 (KJV)**

Chapter Five

Does God Endorse Divorce?

*Jesus said, "Moses wrote this command only as a
concession to your hardhearted ways. In the original
creation, God made male and female to be together.
Because of this, a man leaves father and mother, and
in marriage he becomes one flesh with a woman—
no longer two individuals, but forming a new unity.
Because God created this organic union of the two sexes,
no one should desecrate his art by cutting them apart."*
Mark 10:5-9 (MSG)

The Scripture's theme above conveys Jesus' response
to the Pharisees question whether it is right for a
man to divorce his wife. The ordinances of the
Old Testament did instruct that to be married,
a woman had to be a virgin and whoever took a

virgin in marriage was compelled to be married to her for life, see Deuteronomy 22:13-19.

The law also allowed a man to put away his wife if she was found not to be a virgin in which case, the woman in question was to be stoned to death. In addition, the ordinances of the Old Testament law did make further provisions for divorce, in case a man no longer loves his wife:

> "If a man marries a woman and then it happens that he no longer likes her because he has found something wrong with her, he may give her divorce papers, put them in her hand and send her off."
> Deuteronomy 24:1 (MSG)

A woman who got divorced under this scenario was allowed to remarry to someone else and if that happened, she was never to remarry the man who initially divorced her.

We see that in the context of the Old Testament, the law allowed for divorce as a matter of expediency. But in our theme scripture above, Jesus lets us know that divorce wasn't God's original plan. Malachi 2: 16 (MSG) vividly expresses this point:

> "I hate divorce," says the God of Israel. God-of-the-Angel-Armies says, "I hate the violent dismembering of the 'one flesh' of marriage."

In the New Testament, very few scriptures deal with the issue of divorce. One of those is Matthew 5:32. For too long, many Christians have misinterpreted the scripture in Matthew 5:32 as saying that Jesus endorses divorce in the event of marital unfaithfulness, but that is not exactly what Jesus meant in that scripture. Otherwise, Jesus would be contradicting His own words recorded in Mark 10:5-9 cited above.

As a biblical rule of thumb, no one Scripture contradicts another. That's why the Bible is referred to as the body of revealed truth. To fully understand the import of Matthew 5:32, one need to read it in the context of the preceding verse:

"Remember the Scripture that says, 'whoever divorces his wife let him do it legally, giving her divorce papers and her legal rights'? Too many of you are using that as a cover for selfishness and whim, pretending to be righteous just because you are 'legal.' Please, no more pretending. If you divorce your wife, you're responsible for making her an adulteress (unless she has already made herself that by sexual promiscuity). And if you marry such a divorced adulteress, you're automatically an adulterer yourself. You can't use legal cover to mask a moral failure." Matthew 5: 31-32 (MSG)

Clearly, this isn't a statement of endorsement of divorce on grounds of marital unfaithfulness. Rather, Jesus was addressing two interconnected issues here: (1) the technicalities of the law which the people of His day were using in order to circumvent God's original position against divorce and (2) the consequences of divorce.

Thus, the substance of Jesus' message here is on the fact that a legal divorce certificate handed to a wife might sometimes exonerate the husband from the sin of adultery (if the wife is already guilty of adultery), but Jesus isn't endorsing the legality of divorce. Divorce remains an abhorrent act in God's sight.

In conclusion, God expects couples to remain married for life and Romans 7:2-3 makes clear that the only time a married couple is liberated from the marriage commitment is if one of them dies.

Chapter Six

Problematic Situations

Although God has set out the biblical pattern for marriage as we have seen in the preceding chapters, some folks don't always get it right either due to their ignorance of God's Word or due to stubbornness. Yet, in His infinite mercy, God has also laid out certain principles of correction in His Word.

This chapter addresses some of the problematic marriage situations that arise because one of the parties to a marriage is saved and the other isn't—what has been biblically termed 'mixed marriages.' It also lays out the appropriate conduct to adopt when (1) an unbelieving spouse quits, and (2) when believing spouses divorce and finally provides some biblical rules for remarrying.

Is it biblical for a believing spouse to divorce his/ her unbelieving spouse?

First, it's important to recognize that this scenario might arise because prior to the salvation of one of the spouses, both were already married. It also could be the case that one of the saved spouses has decided to abandon the faith in Jesus Christ—apostasy.

> "For the rest of you who are in mixed marriages—Christian married to non-Christian—we have no explicit command from the Master. So this is what you must do. If you are a man with a wife who is not a believer but who still wants to live with you, hold on to her. If you are a woman with a husband who is not a believer but he wants to live with you, hold on to him . . ." 1 Cor.7:12-13 (MSG)

The above scripture reveals two essential truths regarding mixed marriages. First, the Lord God has no explicit instructions regarding mixed marriages because He does not approve of such marriages in the first place. So in the above Scriptures, the Apostle Paul is applying divine wisdom to these situations.

Second, and interesting to note, is that the above Scripture validates God's original position against divorce. It clearly admonishes the saved man or woman in a mixed marriage situation to hold on to the marriage as long as the unbelieving spouse wants to stay.

This Scripture suggests that the saved spouse is biblically bound to the marriage with his/her unsaved partner until the later decides to quit, implying that the initiative to divorce in this case must originate from the unbelieving spouse.

God's wisdom here is that the saved spouse might eventually bring about the salvation of the unsaved spouse. However, as emphasized in earlier chapters of this book, this wisdom is in no way a tacit approval of marriage between a saved Christian and an unbeliever because God's Word clearly discourages those kinds of marriages.

So if prior to being married, both spouses were unsaved but along the line one of them got saved, the primary responsibility of the saved spouse in this scenario is to help bring salvation to the unsaved partner and to the entire family. Make no mistake, this is a very challenging responsibility for anyone and moreso, to the saved female spouse. This is because the saved wife, although possessing more wisdom than her unsaved husband, still has the obligation to be submissive under the authority and direction of her unsaved husband.

There is a well-known story of how a certain woman's wisdom and submission eventually led to the remarkable salvation of her husband. According to the testimony, the unsaved husband was always antagonistic to the Christian activities of his wife. In particular, he always disapproved of his wife's participation at Christian night vigils. It turns out that on this fateful day, the wife who had been attending a Christian crusade returned home late in the night only to find that her husband would not let her into the house.

After many unsuccessful attempts at the door in that cold winter night, she decided to spend the rest of the night at the door steps of their home. It was only at dawn that the husband decided to let her in. To his greatest surprise, not only was his wife not angry at him, but shortly after she entered the house she went straight into the kitchen to fix breakfast for him. According to the testimony the action of the wife has led the husband to give his life to Christ, and he went ahead later to become a leading evangelist.

In summary, Christian women who find themselves in mixed marriage situations are called to show their unsaved spouses the Christ-like love they can't deny, which will lead to their salvation. Such a task is easier if the woman is very prayerful.

It's important to emphasize here that the woman must do the praying herself: simply hiring prayer warriors from all corners of the planet won't get the job done. Someone may say "but I have been praying for my husband's salvation for decades now but nothing is happening, instead he is getting more hardened. The other day he hid the car keys just to prevent me from attending Church service.

How long should one pray for a loved one in order to get him saved?"

The answer is simple. Ask yourself: what is my true motive for asking for the salvation of my spouse? Is it so that he might fulfill his calling in Christ or is it so that he can be a good husband to me? You see beloved, no matter how long you have been persisting in prayer for something, the *motive* for your prayer matters if you are to obtain the desired results:

> "... You do not have because you do not
> ask. Or you do ask [God for them] and
> yet fail to receive because you ask with
> wrong purpose and evil, selfish motives.
> Your intention is [when you get what you
> desire] to spend it in sensual pleasures."
> James 4:2-3 (AMP)

Therefore, if the true motive for seeking your spouse's salvation is so that he/she can be a good husband/wife to you, then that's a selfish motive and chances are that if you don't repent of that wrong motive in prayer, your unbelieving spouse will die in that state and God will hold you accountable.

That said, after having done all to show an unsaved spouse the way of salvation, if he/she continues to resist and worse still, desires to quit the marriage, so be it! But Christian spouses take note: *you are never to divorce your unsaved spouses even if they resist salvation.* Let the divorce initiative originate from the unsaved spouse, in order for you to be liberated of the marriage (in other words, to be eligible for remarriage). Note that the scripture demands you to live a holy single life for the rest of your life, if you decide to divorce your unsaved spouse, against his/her wishes.

What is the appropriate conduct to adopt when an unbelieving spouse quits?

> "On the other hand, if the unbelieving spouse walks out, you've got to let him or her go. You don't have to hold on desperately. God has called us to make the best of it, as peacefully as we can." 1Cor.7:15 (MSG)

The Scripture above tells us that the man or woman whose unbelieving spouse has walked away is no longer bound by the terms of that marriage. Rather, he or she is free to remarry if he/she so desires.

Notwithstanding the freedom to remarry someone else, the Scriptures show us that there is an appropriate attitude expected of saved spouses even when their unbelieving partners walk away:

"You never know wife: The way you handle this might bring your husband not only back to you but to God. You never know husband: The way you handle this might bring your wife not only to you but to God." 1Cor.7:16 (MSG)

It's important to note in conclusion that under this scenario, should a divorced saved spouse desire to remarry, he or she must comply with the biblical procedure in this matter: which is, to be married only to someone who is likewise saved.

What are the consequences when believing spouses divorce?

"And if you are married, stay married. This is the Master's command, not mine. If a wife should leave her husband, she must either remain single or else come back and make things right with him.

And a husband has no right to get rid of his wife." 1Cor.7:10 (MSG)

First, it's important to recognize that the instruction in the scripture above is to Christians who have professed their faith in Jesus Christ (those who are born-again).

Second, it's an instruction from the Lord Jesus Himself—not the Apostle Paul's instruction, as noticed in the sixth verse of this same chapter. The Lord Jesus commands married Christians to stay married until death do them part.

However, should divorce come in at the request of one of the spouses, the scripture says the spouse who demands divorce must remain single for the rest of his/her life, otherwise he/she should reunite back in marriage. Correspondingly, if the both spouses consent to divorce, they are each compelled to remain single for the rest of their lives; otherwise, they should reconcile and be remarried together again.

As if enough is not enough, the scripture alerts us of an even greater potential consequence of divorce for a man who sends away his wife, over and above the requirement that he leads a single life forever.

In Matthew 5:32 the scripture instructs that if someone else commits sexual intercourse with a divorced woman (who has not previously committed adultery), then the man who divorced her will be guilty of adultery:

> ". . . If you divorce your wife, you're responsible for making her an adulteress (unless she has already made herself that by sexual promiscuity)."

Chapter Seven

Parents' Role in Their Children's Marriage Decision

"Don't marry them: Don't give your daughters to their sons and don't take their daughters for your sons—before you know it they'd involve you in worshiping their gods and God would explode in anger, putting a quick end to you." Deut. 7:3-4 (MSG)

The context of the scripture above refers to the command of God to the Israelites as they were about to enter and possess the land God had promised them. It's important to note that there were seven other races (or nations) in the Promised Land and all of them were bigger and stronger than the Israelites.

Then, the Israelites were the only race or nation chosen by God. As the Israelites were about to enter the promised land, the Lord clearly instructed them to have nothing to do with the seven other races found in that land: they were not to give their children in marriage to people from those other races.

The wisdom being that, soon enough, the Israelites married to those other races would be corrupted by the gods of those other races and consequently, God's anger will be kindled on the Israelites to destroy them. Amazing how God loves His people to the extent of showing them where they could miss the mark and the consequences thereof.

Well someone may say the above scripture referred specifically to the Israelites and not to us the Church of Jesus Christ which now includes everyone, both

Jews and Gentiles. But that's not entirely true. The scriptures show us that the Israelites—which were God's chosen people in the Old Testament—were a type of the Church of Jesus Christ today. To the Israelites, the Lord God said this (notice this scripture is the same as in Deuteronomy 7:6):

> "For thou art a holy people unto the Lord thy God, and the Lord hath chosen thee to be a peculiar people unto Himself, above all the nations that are upon the earth." Deut. 14:2 (KJV)

Notice this: the Lord God also describes the Church of Jesus Christ today as His chosen, special, peculiar people—which is the same description He gave to the Israelites:

> "But ye are a chosen generation, a royal priesthood, an holy nation, a peculiar

people, that ye should show forth the praises of him who hath called you out of darkness into his marvelous light." 1 Peter 2:9 (KJV)

Thus, in God's mind, just as there was only one chosen race against seven others in the days of the Israelites; today there is only one chosen race—the Church of Jesus Christ—against all the other races in the world.

The implication of this is that, the marriage instruction that was given to the Israelite race continues to apply to the Church race today: Christian parents mustn't give their children in marriage to people who are not in the Church race—who do not belong in Zion—as the gods of those other races would corrupt them and consequently provoke God's anger on you.

No one emphasizes this point better than the Prophet Nehemiah:

> Also in those days I saw Jews who had married women from Ashdod, Ammon, and Moab. Half the children couldn't even speak the language of Judah: all they knew was the language of Ashdod or some other tongue. So I took those men to task, gave them a piece of my mind, even slapped some of them and jerked them by the hair. I made them swear to God: "Don't marry your daughters to their sons and don't let their daughters marry your sons—and don't you yourselves marry them! Didn't Solomon the king of Israel sin because of women just like these? Even though there was no king quite like him, and God loved him and made him king over all

Israel, foreign women were his downfall. Do you call this obedience—engaging in this extensive evil, showing yourselves faithless to God by marrying foreign wives?'" Neh. 13:23-27 (MSG)

Besides the corrupting influence of worshiping other gods—which marrying outside of Zion causes—the scripture in Nehemiah 13 above shows us that your children's language will also be corrupted.

In Zion, we have a peculiar language or way of talking that is different from the world's language. For instance, the world frequently uses expressions such as "I'm afraid I might not make it", "I'm sick and tired of this or that," or "You never can tell life is full of ups and downs," and the world finds no problems with this manner of communication. But in Zion, we don't talk like that: we don't talk fear, sickness or defeat because such perverse communication breaches the operation of the Spirit in one's life. That's why we rule and reign over life's circumstances everyday!

The *intra-tribal* marriage requirement within the Zion race is so crucially important to God that He specifically instructed another prophet, Malachi, to warn us of the consequences of marrying alien races: the act desecrates the holiness of God, brings a curse, and leads to the extermination from Zion of whoever does it:

> ". . . Judah has desecrated the holiness of God by falling in love and running off with foreign women, women who worship alien gods. God's curse on those who do this! Drive them out of house and home! They're no longer fit to be part of the community no matter how

many offerings they bring to God-of-the-Angel-Armies." Malachi 2:11-12 (MSG)

I have often heard some "smart" folks try to justify their decision to marry unbelievers on grounds that the rich financial stance of their unbelieving spouse would help in sponsoring the gospel. Such folks aren't certainly conversant of what the Prophet Malachi said above: that by the very act of marrying alien tribes, such Christians are no longer part of the Zion community, no matter how much offerings they bring in!

Finally, Joshua also has a warning for us from the Spirit of God regarding the consequences of marrying outside of Zion. He warns that the Lord God will not come to your rescue when the problems associated with such marriages begin choking your life. Even more frightening, Joshua warns of the risk of one losing his/her place in Zion:

"Now, vigilantly guard your souls: Love God, your God. Because if you wander off and start taking up with these remaining nations still among you (intermarry, say, and have other dealings with them), know for certain that God, your God, will not get rid of these nations for you. They'll be nothing but trouble to you—horsewhips on your backs and sand in your eyes— until you're the ones who will be driven out of this good land that God, your God, has given you." Joshua 23:11-13 (MSG)

I understand that we are living in perilous times and some parents don't have any influence over their children's marriage decisions. Indeed some parents aren't even aware that they are supposed to have a role in shaping their children's marriage decisions. Some attempt to influence their children's choices very late—when these children are already grown up and matured—with disastrous consequences.

Another category of parents aren't even aware that their children are already married. Sad enough! But that's precisely why the Spirit of God prompted me to write this book in order to help current and "would-be" parents avoid the pitfalls of their predecessors.

Christian parents, in particular the fathers, understand that you have a God-given assignment to raise your children in the way of the Lord including, ensuring that they marry only within the Zion race.

Fathers, your household—your wife and children—are your primary mission field. Settle this in your mind that you are the teacher, pastor, evangelist, prophet and apostle in your family. God expects you to be successful in these roles in your primary mission field before you can see meaningful results in your secondary mission fields.

When you train a child the way he should go, when he is grown up he will not depart from it, Proverbs 22:6 says. The problem is that many parents have focused their attention solely on the secular education of their children—sending them to fine schools—but have ignored the training of their children in the fear of the Lord.

So these children grow up without the fear of the Lord in them. Without the fear of God in them, there is also no wisdom because the fear of the Lord is the beginning of wisdom. No doubt you would hear that a brilliant kid, who would have left a lasting positive impact in the world, has shot and killed several people including himself. Proper upbringing of kids in the fear of God would have avoided these kinds of situations.

One cannot overemphasize the importance of paying attention to the spiritual development of children, both formal (for instance, Sunday schools) and informal (done at home by the parents themselves) right from the early ages.

Scientific studies have shown that from the time of pregnancy right up to the age of 4, every child must have received the critical ingredients that are necessary for a proper development of the human brain. This implies that the degree of intelligence of a child, how far he/she will rise on the academic ladder, and consequently, his/her expected earnings in life, are all determined before the child ever attains the age of 4.

Thus, a deficiency in nutrients intake at the very early ages would set the child back for life.

The same applies to the spiritual development of the child. When at the early ages they miss the basic foundations of Christian belief, values and principles, it's going to take the supernatural grace of God to bring them back on track when they are grown up.

My late Dad was a secular teacher but at home, he frequently taught me and my siblings God's Word, in addition to math and science. He regularly ensured that we attended church services. I still remember the monthly Friday prayer night vigils, which I frequently attended as a kid with my Dad and Mom. This solid foundation in Christ that my parents laid in me ensured that I stay the course of my faith in Christ, even after I left home and went to college and later university.

Consistent with this background, I and my wife, Belinda, are now giving our three kids—Fred, Paul and Chrisma—the same sound biblical upbringing in the things of God.

The bottom line here is that, if parents desire to have leverage over their children's future decisions—be it their marriage decisions or whatever—it would have to come from a conscious effort at sound spiritual training of their children while they are still young.

However, if you parents yourselves are not grounded in the things of God, its going to be difficult for you to transfer biblical knowledge that you don't have. My advice in this case is for you to locate a bible-based church in your area and be a consistent member along with your entire family. It is also a wise idea for you the father to try and develop a close relationship with your local pastor, who will be able to equip you to properly function in your God-given assignment in your family.

Chapter Eight

The Consequences of Marital Unfaithfulness

"Honor marriage, and guard the sacredness of sexual intimacy between wife and husband. God draws a firm line against casual and illicit sex."
Hebrews 13:4 (MSG)

The Scripture above clearly shows us the context within which sexual intercourse is tolerated—within the context of a husband and wife. It also warns us that God draws a firm line against sexual conduct outside the marriage framework.

This chapter brings to light and discusses two important consequences of marital unfaithfulness namely—it desecrates the body and offerings of the Christian.

The first important consequence of marital unfaithfulness is that it violates the *sacredness* of the human body:

> "There is a sense in which sexual sins are different from all others. In sexual sin we violate the sacredness of our bodies, these bodies that were made for God-given and God-modeled love, for 'becoming one' with another." 1Cor.6:18 (MSG)

The Apostle Paul explains in the scripture verse above that every sin a man commits is without his body but he that commits fornication sins against his own body.

Understand that our bodies have been paid for with a price—the blood of Jesus—meaning that we no longer own these bodies, but they have become

Christ's property and His Holy Spirit lives in our bodies. For one to commit his body which the Holy Spirit dwells in, to an illicit sexual encounter is sufficient proof of disrespect for the presence of the Holy Spirit.

Further, the Scriptures show that there is more to sex than mere skin on skin. Sex is as much spiritual mystery as physical fact: in sex the two bodies become one. God's wisdom then questions the rationale for pursuing the kind of sex that avoids commitment and intimacy—leaving one lonelier than ever—the kind of sex that can never "become one." Rather, since we want to become spiritually one with the Master, we must only pursue the kind of sex—between husband and wife—that makes us one with God.

In reference to the appropriateness of sex amongst unmarried Christians or between unmarried

Christians and unbelievers, some immature Christians are in the erroneous impression that sex amongst unmarried Christians is tolerable and does not amount to desecrating their bodies—since they each have the Holy Spirit living in them—as opposed to sex with unbelievers. This reasoning probably explains the high rate of sexual promiscuity amongst Christians today. But the truth is that God disapproves of any kind of illicit sex outside the marriage framework, irrespective of whether it is amongst Christians or not.

The second important consequence of marital unfaithfulness is that it desecrates the offerings of the believer:

> ". . . you cover the altar of the Lord with tears [shed by your unoffending wives, divorced by you that you might take heathen wives], and with [your own]

weeping and crying out because the Lord does not regard your offering any more or accept it with favor at your hand. Yet you ask, 'Why does He reject it?' Because the Lord was witness [to the covenant made at your marriage] between you and the wife of your youth, against whom you have dealt treacherously and to whom you were faithless. Yet she is your companion and the wife of your covenant [made by your marriage vows]." Malachi 2:13-14 (AMP)

It is important to underscore the role of offerings in the Old Testament days. Offerings were an essential part of the atonement process for sin (see notably, Exodus 30:10).

Therefore, if the Lord God says that He will disregard the offerings of those who weren't keeping their marriage vows, He was implicitly saying that He will not forgive their sins. However, in the New Covenant, Jesus' blood has atoned for all the sins that we ever committed or will ever commit.

So where does this leave the New Covenant believer? Does the dispensation of grace invalidate the sin in marital unfaithfulness and the consequences thereof? The Scriptures show us that the answer to this question is no. Yes, we live in the dispensation of grace but grace doesn't invalidate the Old Covenant. Jesus made it clear that He didn't come to demolish the law and the prophets but rather to fulfill them:

> "Do not think that I have come to do away with or undo the Law or the Prophets; I have come not to do away with or undo but to complete and fulfill them. For truly I tell you, until the sky and earth

pass away and perish, not one smallest letter nor one little hook [identifying certain Hebrew letters] will pass from the Law until all things [it foreshadows] are accomplished." Matthew 5:17-18 (AMP)

It is therefore clear that marital unfaithfulness desecrates the offerings of a believer whether in the New Covenant or in the Old Covenant.

However, the difference here lies in the purpose for which offerings are given to God: in the Old Covenant, it was primarily for the atonement of sin but for us New Covenant folks, offerings don't serve for the purpose of atoning for sin.

Chapter Nine

Epilogue

This book is a response to a divine call to enlighten the body of Christ and the world at large on the subject of marriage. The timeliness of this book cannot be overemphasized, in the context of the growing divorce rate in the Church today which is fast competing with that in the world. Even more compelling is the scientific evidence linking poverty and many societal vices—such as suicide, crime, drug addiction and school underachievement—to growth in single-parent households in the United States.

I'm logically more perturbed by the above statistical evidence than many folks, given my professional background as a development economist, in addition to my specific calling as an evangelist.

Because such burdens come with responsibility, I have been specifically instructed by the Lord to write this book. Specifically, the Lord wants the world to know that marriage is His idea and God's Spirit inhabits even the smallest details of marriage. The Lord also revealed to me that solidifying the family structure—through properly established marriages—is the key to both poverty alleviation and better functioning communities. If we want to see fewer suicides, less gun violence, less drug addiction and lower school drop-out rates in our communities, we must rethink the basis of our marriage culture / system to re-align it with God's original framework.

I have a final word for parents and spouses. Parents and spouses, please understand that what God wants from marriage is children who are brought up in Godly fear and reverence (Malachi 2:15). Yet, this responsibility is too overwhelming to be fulfilled by a single-parent, in an already stressful world. That's why God wants spouses to properly function together in a marriage set-up, showing the right example for their kids to follow when they grow up.

There is definitely something we can learn here from our ancestor Abraham. In the 18th chapter of the book of Genesis, from the 17th through the 19th verse, the Lord God almighty confesses how He cannot hide anything from Abraham, because of Abraham's heart. In particular, God has observed that Abraham was capable of leading his children and household in the way of the Lord. Because of that God will not dare hide anything that He's doing from Abraham. Isn't that remarkable? So if you long to be connected to divine secrets, the one thing you must do as a parent is to raise up your kids in the way of the Lord.

As parents, one of the things we must consciously do is to be genuinely involved in our children's activities, be it at home or at school. Children learn a lot of many different things at school, on television, through the internet, and from friends; some of which aren't necessarily good for them. That's why parents need to be selective of who their kids' hang out with, what TV channels their kids' watch, which websites they access on the internet, and so on.

I understand that many immigrant parents who are struggling to cope with the hectic work schedules in the United States have allowed their kids' unlimited access to TV and the internet, so as to keep these kids busy or distracted. What a pity to have television raise your kids for you! Parents need to spend quality time with their kids, teaching them amongst other things, the

Word of God. This is the surest way of guarding kids' minds against the corrupting influences of this world. Finally, Christian parents understand that it is your primary responsibility for ensuring that your kids grow in the Lord and eventually become married within the heavenly race.

To folks anticipating a marriage decision, I have this final word. First, please ensure that you have understood your specific calling in Christ. Second, ladies ask the gentleman proposing to you to clearly articulate the vision of his calling in Christ and how you will fit into that vision. You can then weigh his testimony against your own calling to see if there is a match, for the Bible questions how two can walk together if they be not agreed (Amos 3:3).

In conclusion, I'm extremely honored to be a vessel through which the Lord has communicated to you the important truths revealed in this book. I trust that you were blessed by this book. Admittedly, there are several issues surrounding marriage that have not been covered in this single volume and I believe that God will answer your desire to get biblical answers to them in a not-too-distant future.

As I close this book, my heart is burning for those of you who haven't yet made Jesus Christ your Lord and Savior. Dear friend, heaven and hell are real and the Bible warns us that they will be judgment after death. Those who didn't receive salvation in Christ while alive are automatically admitted into hell when they pass away.

Thus, the way to avoid hell is by accepting Jesus Christ as your personal Lord and Savior. Accepting Christ isn't synonymous with either going to church regularly or belonging in any of the denominational churches, even though that is commendable. The scripture shows us how to receive salvation. Salvation is a two-stage process, which begins by believing in your heart that God exists, that He sent His son Jesus Christ to die for us all, and God resurrected Jesus back to life.

If you believe this, that is good, but it is not enough. For devils also believe in God and they so much believe that they tremble (James 2:19), but devils aren't in God's Kingdom precisely because they are incapable of fulfilling the second requirement: confession. Your believing is complete when you confess with your mouth, the Lordship of Jesus. Romans 10: 9-10 (KJV):

> "That if thou shall confess with thy mouth the Lord Jesus, and shalt believe in thine heart that God raised Him from the dead, thou shall be saved. For with the

heart man believeth unto righteousness; and with the mouth confession is made unto salvation."

If you are ready to take this next critical step to salvation, please repeat this prayer to yourself:

O Lord God, I come to You in the name of Jesus Christ. Your Word says: ". . . whosoever shall call on the name of the Lord shall be saved." (Acts 2:21)

I ask Jesus to come into my life. I receive eternal life into my spirit. I declare that I am saved, I am born-again; I am a child of God. I now have Christ dwelling in me and greater is He that is in me than he that is in the world. I now walk in the consciousness of my new life in Christ Jesus, Halleluyah!

Congratulations, you are now a bona fide member of the Church or Zion race and you have now entered into your divine destiny. If you need information on where you can worship or on how you can grow in your Christian faith, please do not hesitate to contact me using the following email address: evangelistjagboragbor@gmail.com

About the Author

Dr. Julius AGBOR AGBOR is an economist by training who received his doctorate degree from the University of Cape Town (South Africa). Previously a research fellow at the Brookings Institution's Africa Growth Program, Dr. Agbor has extensive experience formulating economic policy advice to African governments. A frequent commentator on key media outlets notably, SKY News, the Voice of America, and the BBC, Dr. Agbor's research and commentaries have also featured in scientific journals as well as in *The New York Times*. Dr. Agbor is also a frequent speaker at the U.S. State Department's Foreign Service Institute.

In the spiritual arena, Dr. Agbor holds an advanced certificate in theology and has completed several bible training courses. Since his salvation in Christ on July 28 2003, he has been very passionate about soul-winning and church planting. He has been instrumental in planting a number of Christian churches in Cameroon and South Africa and through personal evangelism; he has led over two hundred folks to Christ. Mentoring young Christians is one of his favorite hobbies and to date, he has a network of over one hundred young people around the world whom he mentors.

He is happily married to Belinda Obi, both originally from Cameroon. They have three biological children—Fred Clancy, Paul Richnel and Chrisma Esther—and an adopted daughter, Dorcas. For additional information, please visit his author website at: www.evangelistjagboragbor.com

CPSIA information can be obtained at www.ICGtesting.com
Printed in the USA
BVOW01s1648241013

334548BV00001B/2/P